SEVEN

imPULSE•press

SEVEN

poems by seven Dorset writers

Sarah Barr
Gill Horitz
Tony Horitz
Paul Hyland
Helen Pizzey
Malcolm Povey
Wendy Lalla Wharam

To Elaine
with love from
Sarah.

imPULSE•press

Published in 2014 by Impulse Press

5 Middlehill Road
Colehill
Wimborne
England
BH21 2SA

email: gill.horitz@talk21.com

Cover design © Gill Horitz 2014

Designed and set by Malcolm Povey
and printed by
The Printing House
London
W1S 1YH

ISBN 978-0-9931346-0-9

British Library Cataloguing-in-Publication Data
A catalogue record for this book is available from
the British Library

Acknowledgements

Some of the poems in **Seven** appeared in the following magazines:

Acumen (Worth Seeing)
Mslexia (Say Yes)
Smith's Knoll (What Lies In The Winter Wood)
South (The Great Wall)
The Clearing (Gin & Morphine)
The Interpreter's House (Bedtime)
The Orange Coast Review (Poulteress)

Thanks are given to their editors.

Contents

Paul Hyland

Gill Horitz

Malcolm Povey

Contributors

Foreword

There are seven of us. Six people sit with me around my table. Each has brought a poem written in the privacy of their own imagination. Someone volunteers to go first, passes copies of their work around and nominates one of us to read it. The appointed person has a quick look at the poem before reading it out loud to the group. The writer hears the poem returned to them in another voice, hears what any reader will confront. After that, the writer reads the poem aloud. We all hear the poem a second time, read as the writer intended it to be heard.

Next, the writer remains silent. That is the strict rule of this table. The rest discuss the poem: its ideas, its feelings, its structure, its music. The writer listens to our honest reactions, our questions, doubts, criticisms and praise. Usually the writer takes notes. Only when we have finished ruminating and talking is the writer allowed to speak. He or she may explain the poem or something in it, or question our reactions, or ask for a comment to be expanded. When the discussion resolves itself, or after about twenty minutes, the next volunteer passes a new poem around the table.

The process is always the same, and different every time, because the poems, the voices around the table, are so distinctive. The process is my version of the method employed by the poet/teacher/critic Philip Hobsbaum (1932-2005) in workshops with many of the most distinguished poets of the twentieth century. It promotes self-criticism; it discourages both back-patting and bitchiness; it rewards rigorous analysis and constructive comment. Finally, it requires us all to be humane and ambitious.

I am fortunate to sit at my table with six writers who are so talented, experienced and generous. Every workshop brings surprises and delights. Together we are seven.

Paul Hyland

Wendy Lalla Wharam

Sky-Walking On Studland Beach

Look, the sky has come down to earth.
In the shallow pools we're walking
through clouds, abseiling, hovering
though there's no wind, no wing-quiver
of poised flight. Just the plosh of trainers
in puddles of light.

It's new moon, spring tide
and the sea is as far out as we are
from all we know or remember,
first-footing it on undiscovered ground,
where recently ocean was.

Sun's low dazzle will soon be gone
and this mirrored sky, keeping us afloat.
It's a balancing act between worm-casts
and a soaking as the tide laps in.

Above the low cliff, yellow blaze fades
behind the skeletal branches of wind-bent trees.
A chill breeze quickens. We shiver in the sudden dark.

Sunday Outing

We're on a Sunday outing
to gawp at the crashed aeroplane,
Mam, Dad and me.
I'm six and scared witless.
Winter sun on flat ploughed land.
Distance endless. Sky enormous.
Before the war, it wasn't the same sky,
clouds harmless as Mam's Monday wash
pegged out to dry.

Not far enough away, tangled twists of metal
wink frantic morse. An acrid smell of burning
and wisps of smoke rise on cold air.
Mam talks of cami-knicks and slips
she'll make from the silky parachute.
Dad's proud, 'Our Home Guard
helped gun the blighter down.'

Across the fields, dark figures come running,
shouts drowned by gull cries.
I'm yanked up short
and we're stood stock still,
as Dad takes his cap off.
It seems a kind of prayer
that ends with Dad's gruff amen,
'Well, we'd best be going then.'

Sitting For Her Portrait Aged Twelve

from a painting by Paula Rego

Round her, the light drapes itself.
Her lips refuse to say cheese,
pout don't-care, dare
the wind to change
to fix that look there.

Mummy sang her lullabies,
pinned a dead butterfly
in the tangled net of her hair,
so she could dance for her Daddy,
his little lamb.

Her white frock crumpled
as wind on water.
Her body's curves two hills
and again two hills. Her valleys,
a centipede's spine,
her life an earth road unrolling
and at the end of the road,
lying in wait
a sour old fish-bones,
in her house made of gingerbread.

She'd touched the untouchable,
in her head the unthinkable.
Through the letter-box mouth
she drew once, tumbled out
what she posted, into the lap
of her pretty pretty dress.
Daddy wore four faces,
his eight arms were everywhere.

Every night Mummy tucked her
under a coverlet crisp as pie-crust,
hid her star-gazey eyes.
No-one told her
there was blood
didn't tell her
that something
had to die.

An Adventure In Dress-Making

'That frock becomes you.'
Mam's Dracula,
mouth bristling with pins.
I hate it. 'You'll grow into it.
Make a lady of you yet.'
You bet? I dared her.

Frock's starched white
clasped tight my budding breasts.
My skin felt paper-thin
as flesh became dress.
Puffed sleeves swallowed
plump arms. Neat frilled hem
gulped down knees, then feet,
as Frock became me.
Mam, gob-smacked,
dropped the scissors
with a clatter.

I smashed into lamp-shades
trashed anti-macassars,
through the window
flew into the night,
an outsize cabbage-white.
My ten bone-buttons popped.
Chimney-pots transformed my whiteness
into sooty black. Mam yelled,
'Come back. Come back.'
I tore my little darts apart,
my seams and stitches ripped
on thorny hedges.
Gussets gaped in muddy ditches.

At last, Mam picked me up
and stood me on the table.
'Where did you get off to then?'
She deftly finished off the hem.
'Amazing what a nice frock can do
for a lump of a lass like you.'

Crazy Jack

plagued all seven chapels in the village
with his deafening halleluiahs
but never the seven pubs.
Was an abstemious man, Jack.

Mam said I must always be nice
to Jack and I was. He showed
me many things, but not the things
I knew he knew, just hinted at.

Crazy Jack collected night-soil
from the privies with his cart
after dark. Old maid's, he said, smelled
sweetest. Always, a rose in his button-hole,
red-spotted hanky in his trouser pocket.
The hanky had gold sovereigns in it,
he had a dog flew an aeroplane.
I saw him. And felt the bumps
in Jack's pocket where the sovereigns were.
But he never touched me, ever, honest, I swear.

Except one night, in a dream
I was in Grandma's outside privy, the double-seater.
I'd just learned to read and read everything,
even the pages of *Old Moore's Almanac,*
spiked on a wire for wiping bums, chanted
the poker-work text on the wall,
Oh Lord hold me up, lest I fall,
before dropping the paper in the deep dark hole.
But I'd not prayed hard enough
for there was Crazy Jack,
I spied him through a crack in the door,
trundling his cart up the garden path. Whistling.

This time, he'd not come to empty the privies.
This time, he'd come for me.

Lost

'A lot of people lose their way in India ... it's a country specially made for that.' Antonio Tabucci

How will I find it
that house called Pearl
in a no-name street
I'm moving to?
'Pearls are notoriously hard
to discover, hence the price,'
my landlord-to-be, Professor Chadhouri,
expounds on the phone to me, in his exquisite English.
I picture him, moving his head waggishly
from side to side, Keralan style.
A gesture that always leaves you, the foreigner,
floundering between a yes and a no.

After one hour's walking in the heat,
I pass Divine Electronics on my right,
the Krishna Bank, then Smart-Quick Eezi-Kleen
and the Zam Zam Kool Bar on my left.
Seeking the shade of a chambatta tree,
I walk baretoed amongst a flame of flowers,
adroitly avoid the over-flowing sewer.
In front of Jesus Scooters a pile of refuse
and a sacred cow or two foraging.
Some skinny black and white goats.
A one-eyed man sells bananas from a cart.
No sign of Pearl.
I feel faint with the high humidity
and the conflicting bouquet of flower
and sewer, incense and vegetable rot.
I pass Divine Electronics for the third time.

It isn't as though I'm not following
the Professor's instructions exactly.
I recall his voice on the phone,
'Do not despair, take heart, dear lady,
do not be surprised if you end up
where you start. Put it down to the circularity of time.
At noon, the sun leaves no shadow, many birds sing
in the forest after dark, invisible. Sometimes, we walk in sand
leaving no footprints.'   Pause.   At the other end of the phone,
only the sound of Professor Chadhouiri's
wheezy breath. Just as I'm thinking we've been cut off
a thin voice whispers, 'Maybe . . . it could be . . . that you . . .
like me, do not want to be found.'

Pole-Tapping

That severe winter of forty-seven
I was still a child confined
between two arms of water,
the Humber and the cold North Sea.
The famous bridge arrived too late for me.
We lived unheeded, stubborn, unaware,
backs to the world.
The heaviest snowfall ever meant
no school, no rules, except the freedom
to walk between great cliffs of snow,
the path the snowplough made.

In the hushed world, telegraph poles
huddled deep in their white fleece
and I'd recall how, in other seasons
I'd lean my ear to the wood,
hear sibillant whisperings I'd know
were the hum of gossip
from those long-ago drowned towns,
Ravenserer and Ravenserodd.
Or when the war was on, to eavesdrop
encoded messages from Hitler's spies,
plans to tunnel under the channel,
that I'd one day, famously, reveal.

Those voices buried deep now
under leagues (I like to think it)
of snow, suffocating, slow, muted,
as field-mice in their winter sleep,
and me, with my ear to the pole
never, ever, quite getting the whole story.

Helen Pizzey

Going Digital

The time no longer exists when shadows
from the church spire crawl into
the crusted knot of an old oak to sleep,
or the sun strikes the dial just so.

Lanes, once thick with warm musk of mottled hide,
are dry of milk sprinkled from heavy teats
and gone is the barn where a needlepoint of swallows
wove its tapestries through gloom-laden rafters.

Beyond the creaking gates of churchyards
and between incessant openings
and slamming shut of doors,
three o'clock, that time called *tea*,
is missing.

Like unfrocked priests, ducks are denied daily
trimmed shavings of cake and bread.

Honey

A summer evening drifts
like a hushed high tide
outside my open window.

Through flimsy partitions
and wafery walls,
murmurs start softly
but build to a roar:

there's a crash
then scrape of chair legs
on laminated floor,
followed by – silence.

I remember wetland hayfields
and daub of roughcast bedroom walls
warm against my curious, young palm,
feeling the vibration from
a hum of clotting bees.

Tomorrow, I'll knock and enter,
take her trembling hand in mine
to soothe it with a knowing squeeze.

'I'm fine,' she'll say, 'really.'

The Ballast Of Cows

Any port in a storm,
like the stall with its heavy cargo,
moored fleet of huge-hulled bodies
listing on invisible tides
of ebb and flow of milking.

Cows puffed dampness
through wet muzzles
pricked with tickly stubble;
slap and swing of their bell-rope tails
was dangling, rhythmic toll.

Their wide-eyed listlessness
steadied me – and
the shifting awkwardness
of their great, maternal bulk.

Within confines of spattered brick
we shared closeness, warmth;
a thickening of skin and bone.

Then, when winter passed, these ships
launched out on fields of liquid green,
tails hoisted, running with the breeze;

the churning of seasons
weathering our hide,
making us watertight,
strong.

Sudden Island

derived from voices broadcast
from Muchelney, Somerset

Wave upon wave of swollen river
swept the tops of grassy dykes
like weapons glinting moonlight,

a flatlands invasion so quicksilver slick
the thatcher was glad of his baby's cry
as water lapped the legs of her cot,
rousing him from sleep.

Breaching thresholds and doors
to depths unseen for at least a generation,
it washed high up white farmhouse walls
last notched in '24. Slurry-sloshed sofas
bumped against ducks that circled wading legs;
swamped drains spewed raw sewage
while party Portaloos bobbed about.

Mail vans gasped, then quit.
Provisions and post arrived by punt
till the farmer cranked-up his Fergie,
hitched a trailer with settees on top
and ferried kids to school.

Later, a barrage of beating wings
swooped on fields flooded by searchlight
moons which perfectly mirrored
poplars marking water's slow retreat –

a still-life scene made eerie and strange
by the unsettling acoustics of peace
as silence became a sounding board
for each unknown, distant voice.

The Mason's Daughter

was fluent in lost languages
of stone:

the inference of marble,
granite's slant directness
and the clean annunciation
of the diction of slate.

Pocketing words and phrases
spalled from weathered headstones,
or the vernacular of pebbles
washed-up from other shores,

she added them singly
to a monumental pile,
a cairn of casually-tossed,
loose remarks and
collected observations

showing where she'd been,
who she'd travelled with –
but not, as yet,
the rough-hewn tongues
of places still to visit.

Poulteress

Over three days and nights her plucked life hung,
limp between two worlds. She was good at wringing
flocks of necks, but with her there was no flapping,
no anxious testing of arms transforming into wings;

just a cooling of moist flesh, a pooling of blue blood
at her fingertips, and dry lips narrowed to a fine beak
of bellows as lungs worked overtime, rasping with effort.
The speckled pallor of her skin was clean-scrubbed, unearthly.

At last she was weary. After a tiny final flurry (perhaps
imperceptibly checking lipstick, her hair in the mirror)
she slipped through some invisible wire
and was gone.

Say Yes

I'd have given anything to be a single raindrop
on the end of Andie MacDowell's soaked lashes
when Hugh Grant asked whether not being
married to him was something she thought
she could possibly do for the rest of her life.

Years later, during a night-time difficult labour,
the ewe moaning pitifully in tune with
the December sleety squall, you hollered
'D'you think maybe getting hitched to a
Welsh hill farmer is a bit of a bad idea?'

'I do,' I said.

Tony Horitz

Home Pleasures

After Brecht

The view from my desk
over trees and roofs, my arms
pressed on its distressed, red
leather top, remembering.

Music filling downstairs rooms
on Saturdays with Beethoven,
Bach, Rachmaninov,
Jazz Record Requests.

Re-reading that dog-eared book
of our son's sayings,
aged three to eight,
still hugging him at twenty-nine.

Lying in bed, you beside me,
hearing an owl hoot, knowing
this is enough,
this is it.

Night of the Dead
for my Czech father

Sizzling schnitzel and stewed sauerkraut
would lure you swiftly through the door once.
After Mum had served you'd wolf it down
and between mouthfuls pronounce
in your Mittel-European tones:
'Almost as good as my muzzer's.'

Last All Souls' Night I tried to summon you -
made a shrine by our fireplace:
familiar black and white photos;
the burgundy and blue neck scarf
you wore in the RAF, which I
keep in my sock drawer; and
an LP of your brother playing cello.

By candlelight, I waited long into the night.
You did not come; but in my head,
as I packed away your things,
I heard a laugh
like the one you used
for mocking irrational tosh.
And I could almost see you.

Neighbours

At night we hear the owl hoot,
the fox bark in the wood,
the traffic sweep by.
But we didn't hear our neighbours die,
or notice they'd gone for weeks.

When Eileen passed, the house stayed dark,
as if it were in mourning, both gardens
filled with weeds, while storms
trashed the wooden fences till
they resembled a crone's mouth –
just two brown-stained teeth left;
so unlike Eileen – always well turned out,
hair coiffed and chiffon-scarfed
above those painted eyebrows
like thin birds' wings sliced in two.
She'd hate to hear about this mess;
not that we spoke much in thirty years,
just that business over her giant leylandii,
which still take away our light –
they survived the winds unscathed,
Eileen'd be pleased to know,
if she weren't dead.

And what of Bill, on our other side?
So deaf these last few years,
we haven't talked to him either –
just smiles, waves, and Christmas cards.
Once, in his fifties, Bill fell in love
with a German woman who lived in France.
He was always smiling then, popping round
with wines he'd brought cross channel.
Though they were rough, we'd talk and laugh,
just like neighbours in *The Archers* do. It was nice.
But when she died from 'The Big C',
Bill never really smiled again.
Now the Big C's got Bill too.

Who'll be next, I wonder? Will it be us? And
when it comes, how will our younger neighbours,
hear the news of our passing? Lying in bed,
will they stop to remember us at all,
as they listen to the owl and the fox in the wood?

Angels

Today a buzzard appeared
above my house-top,
hovering in the clear sky
with wings spread wide –
as if it were an angel
and I the only witness.
When sunlight gilded
the dun feathers, I
felt stirred.

Then came two crows, flipping
and flapping at the angel
like priests, driving it
to a nearby garden,
where it took refuge
in a dead tree.

Strange – a life-long agnostic,
I'm watching the sky more,
now I am sixty,
and mistaking killers
for angels
and crows for priests.

Icarus Complex

Oh, Wayfarer of Waxy Wings,
progenitor of Sinking Feelings,
hear me! I am reeling.
Like you, I aim high in life,
dream I'm graceful as an eagle.
Like you, I'm fatally flawed –
not fused feathers but fumbling
fingers send my hopes tumbling.

Take last week, Icarus,
when, failing to read the signs,
I stretched to draw up a blind,
and welcome the morning light.
My cortical connectors crossed,
I blindly led the blind to crash
on a stone-hearted floor –
and sank to my knees once more.

I'm equally clumsy with cafetieres,
jugs, cups, saucers and plates –
washing up is my nemesis,
a job I've come to dread.
So who's a man to turn to,
if not a fabulous failure like you?
I've consulted all the classicists,
no-one else matches my deficit.

Please, is there a solution, Icarus?
What's that? Oh.
Try Prometheus.

Moonlight In Your Voice

Outside, a full moon,
stares at me through
the un-blinded window.
Dazzled, I stare back; recall
Beckett's advice to actors
rehearsing *Waiting for Godot*
in Berlin or maybe Paris:
'When the moon rises,
speak with moonlight in your voice.'

My silver pen scratches
on clean white paper,
but the dirt-dark words
don't shine; are dead.
Trying to fail better,
I make my mouth moon-shaped,
breathe out.
Ohhhhhhhhhhhhhhhh.

Attachment

Dearest Granny Marketta,
your photo arrived from Prague
by attachment last week.
I love your shiny eyes, Granny,
they remind me of sweet almonds,
your young face is like a moon,
and the thick, dark hair behind,
a Bohemian forest.

I'm sorry I've always imagined you old,
Granny, stooping, branded
with a gold Star of David badge
first sent to Teresienstadt,
then on a cattle wagon to Riga,
Transport Number 0725.
You were a tragic victim.
You were smoke from a chimney.

But now I see you as you really were –
long before I was born, Granny,
long before you perished.
How brave you look, how proud,
Czech woman, wife, mother;
your open lips wondering:
'How long must I stay
still and silent? How long?'

Sarah Barr

The Great Wall

My mother's Mahjong set is neatly packed
in a wooden box with sliding lid.
The ivory and bamboo tiles,
engraved in ruby, azure, jade,
the flowers and seasons,
winds and dragons,
chatter like little birds
when she throws them out on the table.

We build the Great Wall
and for a few childhood moments
attend to this task in harmony.

Like pecking sparrows, we were
tipped into this world of flowers and storms,
and dragons breathing flames.

Baffin Land

I'll never forget that argument
when I dug my heels in over Baffin Land.
I've never been there but can imagine
its rocks and deserted flat stretches,
arctic foxes, wolves, snowgeese
and other birds that don't need trees,
vast skies – white or grey –
the taste of snow and smell of tundra,
ground springy or tough beneath my boots.
A place where new things could start.

Grandma came on her own from Yorkshire
to live with us, a family she barely knew.
She was born in eighteen seventy-nine,
baked us cakes, wore a long, flowered apron.
I'd appreciate her skills now, but back then
it must have been something about
my ten-year-old need to push out, dig down.
As I searched round the house for the atlas,
I suspected – no, I knew – she was right.
Baffin Island not Baffin Land – was a fact.

Family Party

It was something of a celebration
though of what, we didn't really know.
We wondered how to take this invitation.

Scrambling en-route into our creations –
me in the dress with difficult-to-tie bow –
we dreaded this Thames river celebration.

You shrugged into your DJ with casual elation.
It fitted, due to your recent sickness, though
this bug could have scuppered the invitation.

Balloons waved us on deck – airy ovations
for this birthday, family, friendship or other
awkwardly mysterious celebration.

After the rows, the silence, the accusations,
our first thought was just to say no.
But in the end we accepted the invitation.

Swans, willows, locks and lit-up mansions
accompanied us along the ancient river.
It was a September celebration.
We couldn't turn down the invitation.

Istanbul

The call to prayer that made us
close our bedroom shutters
at five a.m. now comes and goes –

one low, one higher pitched lament,
an urgent conversation in the sky
I needn't respond to right now

as we sit on this high-up terrace
among seagulls, red evening roofs,
carved minarets and pale grey domes.

I want to board the Bosphorus ferry,
feel sun and wind sting my face,
reach the farthermost harbour with you

for freshly caught seabass
and tiny cups of undrinkable coffee.
Yesterday, we took the camera

among lawns, tulips and mimosa trees.
But no photograph can keep us
in this place – I mean, really keep us.

Westbourne Grove

Ours was the doorway they had to climb past
on the way to their better flat at the top.
We got to know each other
through conversations about the bathroom,
and wariness of our landlady.
They were Steve McQueen and Sandie Shaw
alias Clive and Thelma, with a baby boy
who playfully bashed my typewriter
on which I was writing a novel
in my spare time. 'This is what I do,'
Clive said, slipping something
between the latch and jamb of our door
then handing me the narrow plastic strip
as if trying to recruit us to his shadow-life
of re-distribution in Westbourne Grove,
'but I never use it on my neighbours.'

As we lay in bed in our secret garden
of peeling ivy wallpaper,
we knew our unused tea-service,
six cut-glass whisky tumblers,
purple candle-wick bed-cover
and notes on Beowulf, and Jurisprudence,
were safe, at least while we lived there.

The Couple Upstairs

I'd like to send a message over the years
to the couple who admired our traditional names
but couldn't believe we'd take the risk
of having a baby with no money.

They were saving up to escape
from our Brixton villa divided into flats,
a condemned slum with damp and mice,
to a new place in suburbia.

On Saturday mornings they larked about
in and out of bed, playing practical jokes
with a hot water bottle and cold alarm clock
making each other shriek.

He rode his scooter to work in The Savoy,
sometimes brought food home in the paniers.
She caught a bus to her job in an office.
One evening, they invited us upstairs

to see their living-room crammed with bread
heaped on every surface – French, soda, round,
glazed, plaited, seeded. How many loaves
did we want? How much could we eat?

He brought us bottles of Chateau Pauillac
he said were leftover from the hotel kitchen.
But after Christmas, the two of them disappeared.
I'd like to thank them again for the bread and wine.

Mostyn Road

It was a bit of a palaver
sharing a decrepit bathroom
with a houseful of tenants.

And so, a scrubbing and rinsing
of the bath had to happen
before either of us dared get in

and we shared the water
that clanked in steaming
but wasn't plentiful.

We soaped our newborn baby
in a plastic bowl in the kitchen sink
and then scrubbed the nappies clean.

It was unbelievably satisfying
pegging nappies up in a long row on the line
to billow out like swans in a fairy tale

flying over our sooty city garden
with its brick walls, leaf-strewn lawn
and hardy unpruned roses.

Paul Hyland

Parachutes
for T.G.

What you found in the marsh
two miles north of Carentan
is translated to your yard
at Asnières, behind the farm.

Laid out there, it might be
an explosion of forest fungi,
not an intricate puzzle
of blanched, deformed metal.

The marshland has sprouted
trees planted since the war,
but you mine for remains
with a miniature digger,

for something you can name:
the crumbs and fibres of a tyre
whose exterior diameter,
you say, matches a Lancaster's;

Air Ministry radio gear; and
half a Packard Merlin engine,
exhaust stubs with outer seams
which, you insist, make it a Mk III.

You do not mention bodies.
In your shady barn you show me
tunics, a torn forage cap with wings,
initials inside a wedding ring

which pinpoint crew and sortie –
6 June '44 – a sweater with the DFM
stitched on, dinghies with orange sails
still bright and printed with instructions.

I handle four creased parachutes
unpacked from their pods: dry,
sleek as embryo leaves, destined
for light and air, never unfurled.

Alexanders
Smyrnium olustratum

The storyteller laid a tile
at his feet on the Dorset cliff.
'That,' he said, pointing down at it,
'is a Roman tile.'

Then he removed a single coin,
a denarius, from his purse.
'This,' tossing it palm to palm,
'is a Roman coin.'

The storyteller leaned forward
and dropped the coin onto the tile.
'That,' cupping a hand to his ear,
'is a Roman sound.'

The storyteller brushed a plant,
black lovage, that favours sea shores.
'This Mediterranean herb
is a bitter plant.'

Native now, named Alexanders,
parsley of Alexandria,
it requires earthing and blanching
like our celery.

The storyteller plucked a sprig
in his teeth. 'Roman coin, tile, sea
sound and this,' he smiled, wincing,
'is a Roman taste.'

Otter

Her bolt-hole
a holt among roots
of alder
of language
wild otter
[Latin] *Lutra lutra*
[Old English] *otr, otor*

derived from the root
of *water*
[Umbrian] *utur*
[Latin] *unda* a wave
of muscle
sinuous water
dives over and under

swirl of bubbles
glint of eyes
flair of bristles
river's skin flexed
the mirror broken
drives down *unda*
crunches eel or perch

flat head
firm jaw
and up into air
breast high
breath caught
utur, otr, otor, oter
water utters otter

Lutra lutra tires
retires
her bolt-hole
a holt among roots
of alder
of language
asleep and alert

Fig
Ficus carica

'Of ripe figs there is much to be said,'
sighed Philia, lying soft and young
abreast the table, 'but let us eat instead,
explore the flesh with our tongues,
our teeth grating agreeably on seed.'

And so we did.

Sitting Beside You

Sitting beside you doesn't mean we touch
and yet a breath, a move, a coded word
or glancing intimacy means as much
sometimes as kissing deeply, loving hard.

So we may sit together, just apart,
sensing the frisson, the same current's strength
that sparked across this gap right at the start;
taking as given its full depth and length.

Distance is calibrated by the heart;
sitting by you does not mean we don't touch.

Road To Childhood

Taking the road with you,
under a bigger sky,
I drive through cypress swamps:
all sheen and green and slime
giving up slender trunks
between angular knees,
the daylight fractured, split
on a surface of dreams
above waterlogged roots.

And it seems you must have
grown up here – where the world
needs to be translated,
always interpreted,
ever explained away –
and not those few miles east
between the rational ponds
of the fish hatchery
where your father was boss.

There, mirrors you gazed at
are wrinkled by the wind;
the levees stretch outwards,
flat as a chequerboard
to the end of the earth.
To Spain, for example.
The waters still fertile
and routinely managed
though your dad is long gone.

The place is deserted,
your childhood home silent.
A neighbour's dog, frenzied,
rushes the hedge and a bird
whose name you can't recall
– twin pennants for a tail –
rides the phone line, waiting
maybe for a break in
opaque, promising cloud.

Gin & Morphine

The vet came from a liquid lunch
to drench the bloated cow
with emulsion and morphine.

I stood firm, bracing myself
against the beast's swollen belly
as the drunken man punctured it

with a cannula under the ribs.
The cow let a small bellow
leak from her throat, while

foul air pissed out steadily
filling the stall with stench
spiked by the vet's breath.

We strained to keep the cow
upstanding, and us on our feet.
I think I slept and dreamt

myself hunched under a hot cloud
of cow, suffering evil weather
and waking intoxicated, aching,

to late sunlight in the yard,
the vet revving his Jaguar
the cow upright and deflated.

Gill Horitz

An Object Lying In Wait

When I think of the past I go in pursuit
and follow a thread to the very end,
but without warning forget what I know
or what I know suddenly runs out.

But an object lying in wait, holds
its own life in the shape it makes,
the way my grandmother's coat
appeared at the back of a drawer
where it hadn't been before,
and I said, let me hold it, quickly!

It took me in its arms and we fell back
onto the bed, and from out the cloth
the exact smell of her blue crepe came,
as though she might breathe again
and I would remember more and more.

What Lies In The Winter Wood

End of day, end of year – and she's thinking what's next,
her head against the pane and the wind slamming the gate.

When she looks up, the trees are moving through the half light
towards her, through snow piled over the vanished road.
Not a single thought holds her back.
All the meanings held by the trees she remembers,
and how their barks can be unrolled and written upon.
No ordinary wood moves like this, and time is short.

Through the holly tunnels she sings a low song to the owl
and the night leans down, savouring her wintry breath.
What will I take from this? she thinks, looking back
as the moon hurries her along. To believe just once
that such a place exists, the imaginary heart
where everything worth moving towards lies.

Birdsong In Budapest

A bird wakes me and I hurry to the window
like being summoned, and in the one tree, so close
it almost touches the glass – the bird,

dove-grey in early light, its little mouth
turning the air with a five-boned tongue,
into a song. And as it sings, along the street

to right and left, the windows gleam and quiver,
and the roofs of the parked cars reflect
its shivery brilliance. Under my feet

the parquet vibrates, and the whole house
moves as the nameless bird returns to earth
what keeps getting lost, a particular thing

to belong to, the song, very old and invisible,
which brings to mind every morning, a reminder
of something small but expressible, I want to find.

All The Different Darknesses Of The World

And one such dark was formed from shadows
reaching as far in as the bedside mat
which sat like a little island on the parquet floor
where we undressed. From the top bunk I looked down
on our earrings signaling in the lamplight, red beads
to crystals, and when we turned our pages
the frame gave little shudders, not frighteningly
but in the way of a reminder: what is granted,
take it, full force. And when my granddaughter
leaned out to scoop air in quick beating motions,
another kind of dark opened in me. Of forgetting
these invisible things: the two of us
in a small boat and the sun not far off.

What's Gone

Still the woods opposite and the crossroads.
But on the corner, Eileen's house gone,

dismantled in a week, and her fir trees
and the nests within, like her children's rooms,

reduced and skipped. But suddenly skies
wide-opened to the west, let evening sun

into our living room, for the first time
as far as the hearth. Some of us will stay

and listen to the forthright bird in the old tree.
And measure our luck against what's gone.

I Thought I Was Grown Up

Something must be going on
with time. I feel it skip a beat,
a small thud in my chest
going hurry, hurry. At night

waiting in the dark
I begin to think of a door,
half open on the unlived years
already coming in. Dawns

beginning earlier and earlier,
and more welcome than before.
A brilliance fills the bedside glass
half full the more I look this spring,

and things appear
never before seen or heard.
Where have they been?
How were they missed?

I thought I was grown up,
but now I expect more
from the way my mind
reassembles living signs.

Colours, folds in nature,
an ordinary lapwing.

Fear Of Being Forgotten

Towards the end of winter, listen –
the bedroom chest groans
when spring wakes the grain.

Inside the wood I look again
at someone's hair lying there,
still the thickest brown just waiting
to be stroked or spoken about.

Round and round I run, consigning
all life's fondest things to fill the chest.
Nothing too insubstantial to be forgotten.

Seasons pass and each spring, more easing
of wood. Each spring becomes the last.

But what if no-one comes, no-one thinks to look?

Malcolm Povey

Bedtime

'Do you know your jimjams
are round your ankles?' I ask,
sat on the crapper warmed
by your bum, then bend
and tug them up, over
your cancer-thin thighs.

'Love's young dream,' you giggle,
flanneling your face, one hand
gripping the rim of the sink,
and then, as you wobble,
'It's funny, the places
you end up.' Scanner.
Wig-shop. Near worn out.

'Yes,' I say, 'Life likes
to remind you how little
you matter.'

To life.

But not to me.

Looking Back

There was a last time we walked the shore
and laughed in the cliff lift and exclaimed
at lizards lounging on hot stone.

But we didn't know it was the last:
neither savoured it nor sighed.

There was your last breath. I witnessed that:
your almost rabbit pucker, tiny exhalation,
leaving me to live, a starving fox,
ghosting beside a dying sea.

Aftershock

On the balcony, clutching
a small bottle of beer
from the mini-bar,
my legs shook.
My God, I thought,
this beer, sipped once,
is strong.

Then, from the bed,
you called, 'Malcolm,
the water in my glass
is tilting from side
to side. I'm scared.'

In the street below
people began to group.
Some crying.

'It's an earthquake,'
I said. You asked
what to do. 'Nothing,'
I said, 'Just see
what happens.'

That was nearly
twenty years ago.

We survived,
with a lively tourist
tale to tell.

Now, there's no more 'we'.
I pick my way
through the rubble of my days.
Earth has swallowed you up.
I quake each day.
Can't blame the booze.

Fuck the tsunami.

I want you back.

Since You Died

Remember Wilf, I mutter,
fighting self-pity.

He must have been about sixty,
tweed jacket neither hip, nor trad,
just saggy. A slight stutter,
when he told us, bumped into
in a café doubled at night
as Lancaster's first disco,
that he'd lived his life alone.
'People moan about marriage,'
he said, 'but I think they lack
the guts to admit being happy.'

So now, I tell myself,
remember Wilf. I had
forty-three years with Jackie,
an improvised dance
to life's changing beat,
hands clasped against knocks,
hugging sudden joys,
till death barged in.

Remember Wilf,
his unpartnered life,
and think yourself lucky.

I was.

But luck, as it always does,
staggered out onto streets of loss.
And remembering Wilf,
who must also be dead,
jacket long gone from the Oxfam shop,
doesn't help.

In My Dream

Last night we made love
intent, absorbed, two scholars
just on the brink of solving
a long-dead language. Metaphor
can't catch it. Let's just say
that, waking in my lonely bed,
last night's learned review
of God-knows-what slipping off
the coverlet, (-let? what's that
when probably not at home?)
I realised my little room
will never again be everywhere,
and, God-knows-why, heard
you say, though four years dead, so clear,
of my tears at *The Grapes of Wrath*,
'And aren't you proud of yourself.
Your tears.' You never were a comfy
duvet. I have to get out of bed,
I'm not sure why, something to do with
thickening my skin, day by day,
to still your voice, forget your touch.
It's what they all expect: friends; family.
But, as long as I'm me, I'll hear you say,
when I showed you my draft of *Sedgemoor,*
though your paintings hung all over Poole,
'You've worked harder than me, Malc,'
in your clear, honest way, sunlight
cleansing my germs of doubt, though
only now it strikes, just how precise
your praise. You didn't say my poems
better than your pics, or, indeed,
if they were any good at all,
but you had your Dad's admiration
for hard work, for scratters, who, though
their efforts came to naught, scratted.

Incident

Watching a beetle scurry
from stab of garden-fork
something longer, yellower,
blurs at the edge of my eye.

Carefully parting fat leaves
of the plant I am cheerfully
murdering, I see a frog, small,
which seems to look trustingly
though maybe just too cold to jump.

I spare its hide, reprieve
the leaves above its head,
hoping to be repaid
in munched-up slugs.

Much later that night, turning
off the too turn-offable match,
I think, could it have been Jackie?
After all, she spent long years teaching
Frog, and it's no dafter than the belief
that the dead sled back into our lives
astride the frames of falling pictures.

No dafter. But the tear that almost starts,
then decides to stay safe in its sac,
is not for the chance you've grown amphibious,
cold, and a little repellent, but
that you haven't. That a frog is just a frog,
a slug a slug, a sheltering leaf a lucky chance
the fork stabbed an inch or two away.

Worth Seeing

There are these two dots of girls
walk down my street, their blue school
blazers too big for them, and their legs so thin
you'd think they'd break. They always chatter,
and, today, one had a Santa cap, red
on her head. Though I hate December,
the month my wife died, the idiocies
of Christmas, no matter how depressed,
or bitter, I feel, when I see those two tots,
bold on the road of their lives, like wrens,
they are so tiny, my heart lifts, and I mind less
being old and ill and alone.

Contributors

Sarah Barr (aka Sarah Steele) is a writing tutor in Dorset and for the Open University. She runs the Wimborne Writing Group. Her poetry has been published in magazines and anthologies. She was a Bridport Prize winner (also Dorset winner) in 2010 and the profiled poet in *South 43*. Her debut novel was longlisted for the Mslexia Women's Novel prize 2013. *www.sarah-barr.com*

Gill Horitz has worked in the Arts for many years in Dorset, from running writing groups and literature events to producing community arts projects. Her poems have been published in various magazines, and one was shortlisted for the Bridport Prize (2011). In 2013, she was one of the judges for the Bournemouth Poet Laureate competition. *www.stateofplayarts.co.uk*

Tony Horitz is a storyteller, playwright and theatre director, mainly working in the educational and community arts field. His last play, *GI Joe in Dorset*, was performed in various Dorset venues in 2013. Living in Wimborne, he has written poetry for many years and loves the inter-active approach of Poetry in Progress. *www.stateofplayarts.co.uk*

Paul Hyland was born in Dorset. *Purbeck: The Ingrained Island* was the first of his seven travel books. His latest is the biographical *Ralegh's Last Journey*. His best-selling primer *Getting Into Poetry* is widely acclaimed. *Art of the Impossible* contains new work and poems selected from five previous collections. He is also a professional magician. *www.artoftheimpossible.com*

Helen Pizzey has had poetry published in various magazines and anthologies. Her poems have been set for large-scale choral/orchestral works, including for the Opening of the Derry Peace Bridge and a commemoration of RMS Titanic broadcast on Radio 3. She lives near Wareham and is Assistant Editor of PURBECK!

Malcolm Povey lives in Bournemouth and used to lecture in English at Bournemouth University. His poems have been published widely in magazines and anthologies. His collection *Sedgemoor* was published by Smokestack Books in 2006. The poems published in **Seven** will feature in his next collection, *Missing*.

Wendy Lalla Wharam is the author of several children's books and has written poetry all her life, but until **Seven** has never sought publication. She has had a varied career as painter, puppeteer, storyteller, actor and as Punch & Judy Prof on Swanage Beach. Living in a village in Kerala in her seventies and studying Kathakali theatre has been life-changing.